ISBN: 9781407649467

Published by:
HardPress Publishing
8345 NW 66TH ST #2561
MIAMI FL 33166-2626

Email: info@hardpress.net
Web: http://www.hardpress.net

Synge and the Ireland of His Time

by

William Butler Yeats

TABLE OF CONTENTS

PREFACE

At times during Synge's last illness, Lady Gregory and I would speak of his work and always find some pleasure in the thought that unlike ourselves, who had made our experiments in public, he would leave to the world nothing to be wished away-- nothing that was not beautiful or powerful in itself, or necessary as an expression of his life and thought. When he died we were in much anxiety, for a letter written before his last illness, and printed in the selection of his poems published at the Cuala Press, had shown that he was anxious about the fate of his manuscripts and scattered writings. On the evening of the night he died he had asked that I might come to him the next day; and my diary of the days following his death shows how great was our anxiety. Presently however, all seemed to have come right, for the Executors sent me the following letter that had been found among his papers, and promised to carry out his wishes.

'May 4th, 1908

'Dear Yeats,

'This is only to go to you if anything should go wrong with me under the operation or after it. I am a little bothered about my 'papers.' I have a certain amount of verse that I think would be worth preserving, possibly also the 1st and 3rd acts of 'Deirdre,' and then I have a lot of Kerry and Wicklow articles that would go together into a book. The other early stuff I wrote I have kept as a sort of curiosity, but I am anxious that it should not get into print. I wonder could you get someone--say ... who is now in Dublin to go through them for you and do whatever you and Lady Gregory think desirable. It is rather a hard thing to ask you but I do not want my good things destroyed or my bad things printed rashly-- especially a morbid thing about a mad fiddler in Paris which I hate. Do what you can--Good luck.

'J.M. Synge'

In the summer of 1909, the Executors sent me a large bundle of papers, cuttings from newspapers and magazines, manuscript and typewritten prose and verse, put together and annotated by Synge himself before his last illness. I spent a portion of each day for weeks reading and re-reading early dramatic writing, poems, essays, and so forth, and with the exception of ninety pages which have been published without my consent, made consulting Lady Gregory from time to time the Selection of his work published by Messrs. Maunsel. It is because of these ninety pages, that neither Lady Gregory's name nor mine appears in any of the books, and that the Introduction which I now publish, was withdrawn by me after it had been advertised by the publishers. Before the publication of the books the Executors discovered a scrap of paper with a sentence by J.M. Synge saying that Selections might be taken from his Essays on the Congested Districts. I do not know if this was written before his letter to me, which made no mention of them, or contained his final directions. The matter is unimportant, for the publishers decided to ignore my offer to select as well as my original decision to reject, and for this act of theirs they have given me no reasons except reasons of convenience, which neither Lady Gregory nor I could accept.

W.B. Yeats.

J.M. SYNGE AND THE
IRELAND OF HIS TIME

On Saturday, January 26th, 1907, I was lecturing in Aberdeen, and when my lecture was over I was given a telegram which said, 'Play great success.' It had been sent from Dublin after the second Act of 'The Playboy of the Western World,' then being performed for the first time. After one in the morning, my host brought to my bedroom this second telegram, 'Audience broke up in disorder at the word shift.' I knew no more until I got the Dublin papers on my way from Belfast to Dublin on Tuesday morning. On the Monday night no word of the play had been heard. About forty young men had sat on the front seats of the pit, and stamped and shouted and blown trumpets from the rise to the fall of the curtain. On the Tuesday night also the forty young men were there. They wished to silence what they considered a slander upon Ireland's womanhood. Irish women would never sleep under the same roof with a young man without a chaperon, nor admire a murderer, nor use a word like 'shift;' nor could anyone recognise the country men and women of Davis and Kickham in these poetical, violent, grotesque persons, who used the name of God so freely, and spoke of all things that hit their fancy.

A patriotic journalism which had seen in Synge's capricious imagination the enemy of all it would have young men believe, had for years prepared for this hour, by that which is at once the greatest and most ignoble power of journalism, the art of repeating a name again and again with some ridiculous or evil association. The preparation had begun after the first performance of 'The Shadow of the Glen,' Synge's first play, with an assertion made in ignorance but repeated in dishonesty, that he had taken his fable and his characters, not from his own mind nor that profound knowledge of cot and curragh he was admitted to possess, but 'from a writer of the Roman decadence.' Some spontaneous dislike had been but natural, for genius like his can but slowly, amid what it has of harsh and strange, set forth the nobility of its beauty, and the depth of its compassion; but the frenzy that would have silenced his master-work was, like most violent things artificial, the defence of virtue by those that have but little, which is the pomp and gallantry of journalism and its right to govern the world.

As I stood there watching, knowing well that I saw the dissolution of a school of patriotism that held sway over my youth, Synge came and stood beside me, and said, 'A young doctor has just told me that he can hardly keep himself from jumping on to a seat, and pointing out in that howling mob those whom he is treating for venereal disease.'

II.

Thomas Davis, whose life had the moral simplicity which can give to actions the lasting influence that style alone can give to words, had understood that a country which has no national institutions must show its young men images for the affections, although they be but diagrams of what it should be or may be. He and his school imagined the Soldier, the Orator, the Patriot, the Poet, the Chieftain, and above all the Peasant; and these, as celebrated in essay and songs and stories, possessed so many virtues that no matter how England, who as Mitchell said 'had the ear of the world,' might slander us, Ireland, even though she could not come at the world's other ear, might go her way unabashed. But ideas and images which have to be understood and loved by large numbers of people, must appeal to no rich personal experience, no patience of study, no delicacy of sense; and if at rare moments some 'Memory of the Dead' can take its strength from one; at all other moments manner and matter will be rhetorical, conventional, sentimental; and language, because it is carried beyond life perpetually, will be as wasted as the thought, with unmeaning pedantries and silences, and a dread of all that has salt and savour. After a while, in a land that has given itself to agitation over-much, abstract thoughts are raised up between men's minds and Nature, who never does the same thing twice, or makes one man like another, till minds, whose patriotism is perhaps great enough to carry them to the scaffold, cry down natural impulse with the morbid persistence of minds unsettled by some fixed idea. They are preoccupied with the nation's future, with heroes, poets, soldiers, painters, armies, fleets, but only as these things are understood by a child in a national school, while a secret feeling that what is so unreal needs continual defence makes them bitter and restless. They are like some state which has only paper money, and seeks by punishments to make it buy whatever gold can buy. They no longer love, for only life is loved, and at last, a generation is like an hysterical woman who will make unmeasured accusations and believe impossible things, because of some logical deduction from a solitary thought which has turned a portion of her mind to stone.

III.

Even if what one defends be true, an attitude of defence, a continual apology, whatever the cause, makes the mind barren because it kills intellectual innocence; that delight in what is unforeseen, and in the mere spectacle of the world, the mere drifting hither and thither that must come before all true thought and emotion. A zealous Irishman, especially if he lives much out of Ireland, spends his time in a never-ending argument about Oliver Cromwell, the Danes, the penal laws, the rebellion of 1798, the famine, the Irish peasant, and ends by substituting a traditional casuistry for a country; and if he be a Catholic, yet another casuistry that has professors, schoolmasters, letter-writing priests, and the authors of manuals to make the meshes fine, comes between him and English literature, substituting arguments and hesitations for the excitement at the first reading of the great poets which should be a sort of violent imaginative puberty. His hesitations and arguments may have been right, the Catholic philosophy may be more profound than Milton's morality, or Shelley's vehement vision; but none the less do we lose life by losing that recklessness Castiglione thought necessary even in good manners, and offend our Lady Truth, who would never, had she desired an anxious courtship, have digged a well to be her parlour.

I admired though we were always quarrelling on some matter, J.F. Taylor, the orator, who died just before the first controversy over these plays. It often seemed to me that when he spoke Ireland herself had spoken, one got that sense of surprise that comes when a man has said what is unforeseen because it is far from the common thought, and yet obvious because when it has been spoken, the gate of the mind seems suddenly to roll back and reveal forgotten sights and let loose lost passions. I have never heard him speak except in some Irish literary or political society, but there at any rate, as in conversation, I found a man whose life was a ceaseless reverie over the religious and political history of Ireland. He saw himself pleading for his country before an invisible jury, perhaps of the great dead, against traitors at home and enemies abroad, and a sort of frenzy in his voice and the moral elevation of his thoughts gave him for the moment style and music. One asked oneself again and again, 'Why is not this man an artist, a man of genius, a creator of some kind?' The other day under the influence of memory, I read through his one book, a life of Owen Roe O'Neill, and found there no sentence detachable from its context because of wisdom or beauty. Everything was argued from a premise; and wisdom, and style, whether in life or letters come from the presence of what is self-evident, from that which requires but statement, from what Blake called 'naked beauty displayed.' The sense of what was unforeseen and obvious, the rolling backward of the gates had gone with the living voice, with the nobility of will that made one understand what he saw and felt in what was now but argument and logic. I found myself in the presence of a mind like some noisy and powerful machine, of thought that was no

3

part of wisdom but the apologetic of a moment, a woven thing, no intricacy of leaf and twig, of words with no more of salt and of savour than those of a Jesuit professor of literature, or of any other who does not know that there is no lasting writing which does not define the quality, or carry the substance of some pleasure. How can one, if one's mind be full of abstractions and images created not for their own sake but for the sake of party, even if there were still the need, find words that delight the ear, make pictures to the mind's eye, discover thoughts that tighten the muscles, or quiver and tingle in the flesh, and stand like St. Michael with the trumpet that calls the body to resurrection?

IV.

Young Ireland had taught a study of our history with the glory of Ireland for event, and this for lack, when less than Taylor studied, of comparison with that of other countries wrecked the historical instinct. An old man with an academic appointment, who was a leader in the attack upon Synge, sees in the 11th century romance of Deirdre a re-telling of the first five act tragedy outside the classic languages, and this tragedy from his description of it was certainly written on the Elizabethan model; while an allusion to a copper boat, a marvel of magic like Cinderella's slipper, persuades him that the ancient Irish had forestalled the modern dockyards in the making of metal ships. The man who doubted, let us say, our fabulous ancient kings running up to Adam, or found but mythology in some old tale, was as hated as if he had doubted the authority of Scripture. Above all no man was so ignorant, that he had not by rote familiar arguments and statistics to drive away amid familiar applause, all those had they but found strange truth in the world or in their mind, whose knowledge has passed out of memory and become an instinct of hand or eye. There was no literature, for literature is a child of experience always, of knowledge never; and the nation itself, instead of being a dumb struggling thought seeking a mouth to utter it or hand to show it, a teeming delight that would re-create the world, had become, at best, a subject of knowledge.

V.

Taylor always spoke with confidence though he was no determined man, being easily flattered or jostled from his way; and this, putting as it were his fiery heart into his mouth made him formidable. And I have noticed that all those who speak the thoughts of many, speak confidently, while those who speak their own thoughts are hesitating and timid, as though they spoke out of a mind and body grown sensitive to the edge of bewilderment among many impressions. They speak to us that we may give them certainty, by seeing what they have seen; and so it is, that enlargement of experience does not come from those oratorical thinkers, or from those decisive rhythms that move large numbers of men, but from writers that seem by contrast as feminine as the soul when it explores in Blake's picture the recesses of the grave, carrying its faint lamp trembling and astonished; or as the Muses who are never pictured as one-breasted amazons, but as women needing protection. Indeed, all art which appeals to individual man and awaits the confirmation of his senses and his reveries, seems when arrayed against the moral zeal, the confident logic, the ordered proof of journalism, a trifling, impertinent, vexatious thing, a tumbler who has unrolled his carpet in the way of a marching army.

VI.

I attack things that are as dear to many as some holy image carried hither
and thither by some broken clan, and can but say that I have felt in my body the
affections I disturb, and believed that if I could raise them into contemplation I
would make possible a literature, that finding its subject-matter all ready in men's
minds would be, not as ours is, an interest for scholars, but the possession of a
people. I have founded societies with this aim, and was indeed founding one in Paris
when I first met with J.M. Synge, and I have known what it is to be changed by that
I would have changed, till I became argumentative and unmannerly, hating men even
in daily life for their opinions. And though I was never convinced that the anatomies
of last year's leaves are a living forest, or thought a continual apologetic could do
other than make the soul a vapour and the body a stone; or believed that literature
can be made by anything but by what is still blind and dumb within ourselves, I have
had to learn how hard in one who lives where forms of expression and habits of
thought have been born, not for the pleasure of begetting but for the public good, is
that purification from insincerity, vanity, malignity, arrogance, which is the discovery
of style. But it became possible to live when I had learnt all I had not learnt in
shaping words, in defending Synge against his enemies, and knew that rich energies,
fine, turbulent or gracious thoughts, whether in life or letters, are but love-children.

VII.

Synge seemed by nature unfitted to think a political thought, and with the exception of one sentence, spoken when I first met him in Paris, that implied some sort of nationalist conviction, I cannot remember that he spoke of politics or showed any interest in men in the mass, or in any subject that is studied through abstractions and statistics. Often for months together he and I and Lady Gregory would see no one outside the Abbey Theatre, and that life, lived as it were in a ship at sea, suited him, for unlike those whose habit of mind fits them to judge of men in the mass, he was wise in judging individual men, and as wise in dealing with them as the faint energies of ill-health would permit; but of their political thoughts he long understood nothing. One night when we were still producing plays in a little hall, certain members of the Company told him that a play on the Rebellion of '98 would be a great success. After a fortnight he brought them a scenario which read like a chapter out of Rabelais. Two women, a Protestant and a Catholic, take refuge in a cave, and there quarrel about religion, abusing the Pope or Queen Elizabeth and Henry VIII, but in low voices, for the one fears to be ravished by the soldiers, the other by the rebels. At last one woman goes out because she would sooner any fate than such wicked company. Yet, I doubt if he would have written at all if he did not write of Ireland, and for it, and I know that he thought creative art could only come from such preoccupation. Once, when in later years, anxious about the educational effect of our movement, I proposed adding to the Abbey Company a second Company to play international drama, Synge, who had not hitherto opposed me, thought the matter so important that he did so in a formal letter.

I had spoken of a German municipal theatre as my model, and he said that the municipal theatres all over Europe gave fine performances of old classics but did not create (he disliked modern drama for its sterility of speech, and perhaps ignored it) and that we would create nothing if we did not give all our thoughts to Ireland. Yet in Ireland he loved only what was wild in its people, and in 'the grey and wintry sides of many glens.' All the rest, all that one reasoned over, fought for, read of in leading articles, all that came from education, all that came down from Young Ireland--though for this he had not lacked a little sympathy--first wakened in him perhaps that irony which runs through all he wrote, but once awakened, he made it turn its face upon the whole of life. The women quarrelling in the cave would not have amused him, if something in his nature had not looked out on most disputes, even those wherein he himself took sides, with a mischievous wisdom. He told me once that when he lived in some peasant's house, he tried to make those about him forget that he was there, and it is certain that he was silent in any crowded room. It is possible that low vitality helped him to be observant and contemplative, and made him dislike, even in solitude, those thoughts which unite us to others, much as we all dislike, when fatigue or illness has sharpened the nerves, hoardings covered with advertisements, the fronts of big theatres, big London hotels, and all architecture which has been made to impress the crowd. What blindness did for Homer, lameness for Hephaestus, asceticism for any saint you will, bad health did for him by making him ask no more of life than that it should keep him living, and above all perhaps by concentrating his imagination upon one thought, health itself. I think that all noble things are the result of warfare; great nations and classes, of warfare in the visible world, great poetry and philosophy, of invisible warfare, the division of a mind within itself, a victory, the sacrifice of a man to himself. I am certain that my friend's noble art, so full of passion and heroic beauty, is the victory of a man who in poverty and sickness created from the delight of expression, and in the contemplation that is born of the minute and delicate arrangement of images, happiness, and health of mind. Some early poems have a morbid melancholy, and he himself spoke of early work he had destroyed as morbid, for as yet the craftmanship was not fine enough to bring the artist's joy which is of one substance with that of sanctity. In one poem he waits at some street corner for a friend, a woman perhaps, and while he waits and gradually understands that nobody is coming, sees two funerals and shivers at the future; and in another written on his 25th birthday, he wonders if the 25 years to come shall be as evil as those gone by. Later on, he can see himself as but a part of the spectacle of the world and mix into all he sees that flavour of extravagance, or of humour, or of philosophy, that makes one understand that he contemplates even his own death as if it were another's, and finds in his own destiny but as it were a projection through a burning glass of that general to men. There is in the creative joy an acceptance of what life brings, because we have understood the beauty of what it brings, or a hatred of death for what it takes away, which arouses within us, through some sympathy perhaps with all other men, an energy so noble, so powerful, that we laugh aloud and mock, in the terror or the sweetness of our exaltation, at death and oblivion.

In no modern writer that has written of Irish life before him, except it may be Miss Edgeworth in 'Castle Rackrent,' was there anything to change a man's thought about the world or stir his moral nature, for they but play with pictures, persons, and events, that whether well or ill observed are but an amusement for the mind where it escapes from meditation, a child's show that makes the fables of his art as significant by contrast as some procession painted on an Egyptian wall; for in these fables, an intelligence, on which the tragedy of the world had been thrust in so few years, that Life had no time to brew her sleepy drug, has spoken of the moods that are the expression of its wisdom. All minds that have a wisdom come of tragic reality seem morbid to those that are accustomed to writers who have not faced reality at all; just as the saints, with that Obscure Night of the Soul, which fell so certainly that they numbered it among spiritual states, one among other ascending steps, seem morbid to the rationalist and the old-fashioned Protestant controversialist. The thought of journalists, like that of the Irish novelists, is neither healthy nor unhealthy, for it has not risen to that state where either is possible, nor should we call it happy; for who would have sought happiness, if happiness were not the supreme attainment of man, in heroic toils, in the cell of the ascetic, or imagined it above the cheerful newspapers, above the clouds?

VIII.

Not that Synge brought out of the struggle with himself any definite philosophy, for philosophy in the common meaning of the word is created out of an anxiety for sympathy or obedience, and he was that rare, that distinguished, that most noble thing, which of all things still of the world is nearest to being sufficient to itself, the pure artist. Sir Philip Sidney complains of those who could hear 'sweet tunes' (by which he understands could look upon his lady) and not be stirred to 'ravishing delight.'

'Or if they do delight therein, yet are so closed with wit,
As with sententious lips to set a title vain on it;
Oh let them hear these sacred tunes, and learn in Wonder's schools
To be, in things past bonds of wit, fools if they be not fools!'

Ireland for three generations has been like those churlish logicians. Everything is argued over, everything has to take its trial before the dull sense and the hasty judgment, and the character of the nation has so changed that it hardly keeps but among country people, or where some family tradition is still stubborn, those lineaments that made Borrow cry out as he came from among the Irish monks, his friends and entertainers for all his Spanish Bible scattering, 'Oh, Ireland, mother of the bravest soldiers and of the most beautiful women!' It was as I believe, to seek that old Ireland which took its mould from the duellists and scholars of the 18th century and from generations older still, that Synge returned again and again to Aran, to Kerry, and to the wild Blaskets.

IX.

'When I got up this morning' he writes, after he had been a long time in Innismaan, 'I found that the people had gone to Mass and latched the kitchen door from the outside, so that I could not open it to give myself light.

'I sat for nearly an hour beside the fire with a curious feeling that I should be quite alone in this little cottage. I am so used to sitting here with the people that I have never felt the room before as a place where any man might live and work by himself. After a while as I waited, with just light enough from the chimney to let me see the rafters and the greyness of the walls, I became indescribably mournful, for I felt that this little corner on the face of the world, and the people who live in it, have a peace and dignity from which we are shut for ever.' This life, which he describes elsewhere as the most primitive left in Europe, satisfied some necessity of his nature. Before I met him in Paris he had wandered over much of Europe, listening to stories in the Black Forest, making friends with servants and with poor people, and this from an aesthetic interest, for he had gathered no statistics, had no money to give, and cared nothing for the wrongs of the poor, being content to pay for the pleasure of eye and ear with a tune upon the fiddle. He did not love them the better because they were poor and miserable, and it was only when he found Innismaan and the Blaskets, where there is neither riches nor poverty, neither what he calls 'the nullity of the rich' nor 'the squalor of the poor' that his writing lost its old morbid brooding, that he found his genius and his peace. Here were men and women who under the weight of their necessity lived, as the artist lives, in the presence of death and childhood, and the great affections and the orgiastic moment when life outleaps its limits, and who, as it is always with those who have refused or escaped the trivial and the temporary, had dignity and good manners where manners mattered. Here above all was silence from all our great orator took delight in, from formidable men, from moral indignation, from the 'sciolist' who 'is never sad,' from all in modern life that would destroy the arts; and here, to take a thought from another playwright of our school, he could love Time as only women and great artists do and need never sell it.

X.

As I read 'The Aran Islands' right through for the first time since he showed it me in manuscript, I come to understand how much knowledge of the real life of Ireland went to the creation of a world which is yet as fantastic as the Spain of Cervantes. Here is the story of 'The Playboy,' of 'The Shadow of the Glen;' here is the 'ghost on horseback' and the finding of the young man's body of 'Riders to the Sea,' numberless ways of speech and vehement pictures that had seemed to owe nothing to observation, and all to some overflowing of himself, or to some mere necessity of dramatic construction. I had thought the violent quarrels of 'The Well of the Saints' came from his love of bitter condiments, but here is a couple that quarrel all day long amid neighbours who gather as for a play. I had defended the burning of Christy Mahon's leg on the ground that an artist need but make his characters self-consistent, and yet, that too was observation, for 'although these people are kindly towards each other and their children, they have no sympathy for the suffering of animals, and little sympathy for pain when the person who feels it is not in danger.' I had thought it was in the wantonness of fancy Martin Dhoul accused the smith of plucking his living ducks, but a few lines further on, in this book where moral indignation is unknown, I read, 'Sometimes when I go into a cottage, I find all the women of the place down on their knees plucking the feathers from live ducks and geese.'

He loves all that has edge, all that is salt in the mouth, all that is rough to the hand, all that heightens the emotions by contest, all that stings into life the sense of tragedy; and in this book, unlike the plays where nearness to his audience moves him to mischief, he shows it without thought of other taste than his. It is so constant, it is all set out so simply, so naturally, that it suggests a correspondence between a lasting mood of the soul and this life that shares the harshness of rocks and wind. The food of the spiritual-minded is sweet, an Indian scripture says, but passionate minds love bitter food. Yet he is no indifferent observer, but is certainly kind and sympathetic to all about him. When an old and ailing man, dreading the coming winter, cries at his leaving, not thinking to see him again; and he notices that the old man's mitten has a hole in it where the palm is accustomed to the stick, one knows that it is with eyes full of interested affection as befits a simple man and not in the curiosity of study. When he had left the Blaskets for the last time, he travelled with a lame pensioner who had drifted there, why heaven knows, and one morning having missed him from the inn where they were staying, he believed he had gone back to the island and searched everywhere and questioned everybody, till he understood of a sudden that he was jealous as though the island were a woman.

The book seems dull if you read much at a time, as the later Kerry essays do not, but nothing that he has written recalls so completely to my senses the man as he was in daily life; and as I read, there are moments when every line of his face, every inflection of his voice, grows so clear in memory that I cannot realize that he is dead. He was no nearer when we walked and talked than now while I read these unarranged, unspeculating pages, wherein the only life he loved with his whole heart reflects itself as in the still water of a pool. Thought comes to him slowly, and only after long seemingly unmeditative watching, and when it comes, (and he had the same character in matters of business) it is spoken without hesitation and never changed. His conversation was not an experimental thing, an instrument of research, and this made him silent; while his essays recall events, on which one feels that he pronounces no judgment even in the depth of his own mind, because the labour of Life itself had not yet brought the philosophic generalization, which was almost as much his object as the emotional generalization of beauty. A mind that generalizes rapidly, continually prevents the experience that would have made it feel and see deeply, just as a man whose character is too complete in youth seldom grows into any energy of moral beauty. Synge had indeed no obvious ideals, as these are understood by young men, and even as I think disliked them, for he once complained to me that our modern poetry was but the poetry 'of the lyrical boy,' and this lack makes his art have a strange wildness and coldness, as of a man born in some far-off spacious land and time.

XI.

There are artists like Byron, like Goethe, like Shelley, who have impressive personalities, active wills and all their faculties at the service of the will; but he belonged to those who like Wordsworth, like Coleridge, like Goldsmith, like Keats, have little personality, so far as the casual eye can see, little personal will, but fiery and brooding imagination. I cannot imagine him anxious to impress, or convince in any company, or saying more than was sufficient to keep the talk circling. Such men have the advantage that all they write is a part of knowledge, but they are powerless before events and have often but one visible strength, the strength to reject from life and thought all that would mar their work, or deafen them in the doing of it; and only this so long as it is a passive act. If Synge had married young or taken some profession, I doubt if he would have written books or been greatly interested in a movement like ours; but he refused various opportunities of making money in what must have been an almost unconscious preparation. He had no life outside his imagination, little interest in anything that was not its chosen subject. He hardly seemed aware of the existence of other writers. I never knew if he cared for work of mine, and do not remember that I had from him even a conventional compliment, and yet he had the most perfect modesty and simplicity in daily intercourse, self-assertion was impossible to him. On the other hand, he was useless amidst sudden events. He was much shaken by the Playboy riot; on the first night confused and excited, knowing not what to do, and ill before many days, but it made no difference in his work. He neither exaggerated out of defiance nor softened out of timidity. He wrote on as if nothing had happened, altering 'The Tinker's Wedding' to a more unpopular form, but writing a beautiful serene 'Deirdre,' with, for the first time since his 'Riders to the Sea,' no touch of sarcasm or defiance. Misfortune shook his physical nature while it left his intellect and his moral nature untroubled. The external self, the mask, the persona was a shadow, character was all.

XII.

He was a drifting silent man full of hidden passion, and loved wild islands, because there, set out in the light of day, he saw what lay hidden in himself. There is passage after passage in which he dwells upon some moment of excitement. He describes the shipping of pigs at Kilronan on the North Island for the English market: 'when the steamer was getting near, the whole drove was moved down upon the slip and the curraghs were carried out close to the sea. Then each beast was caught in its turn and thrown on its side, while its legs were hitched together in a single knot, with a tag of rope remaining, by which it could be carried.

Probably the pain inflicted was not great, yet the animals shut their eyes and shrieked with almost human intonations, till the suggestion of the noise became so intense that the men and women who were merely looking on grew wild with excitement, and the pigs waiting their turn foamed at the mouth and tore each other with their teeth.

After a while there was a pause. The whole slip was covered with amass of sobbing animals, with here and there a terrified woman crouching among the bodies and patting some special favourite, to keep it quiet while the curraghs were being launched. Then the screaming began again while the pigs were carried out and laid in their places, with a waistcoat tied round their feet to keep them from damaging the canvas. They seemed to know where they were going, and looked up at me over the gunnel with an ignoble desperation that made me shudder to think that I had eaten this whimpering flesh. When the last curragh went out, I was left on the slip with a band of women and children, and one old boar who sat looking out over the sea.

The women were over-excited, and when I tried to talk to them they crowded round me and began jeering and shrieking at me because I am not married. A dozen screamed at a time, and so rapidly that I could not understand all they were saying, yet I was able to make out that they were taking advantage of the absence of their husbands to give me the full volume of their contempt. Some little boys who were listening threw themselves down, writhing with laughter among the sea-weed, and the young girls grew red and embarrassed and stared down in the surf.' The book is full of such scenes. Now it is a crowd going by train to the Parnell celebration, now it is a woman cursing her son who made himself a spy for the police, now it is an old woman keening at a funeral. Kindred to his delight in the harsh grey stones, in the hardship of the life there, in the wind and in the mist, there is always delight in every moment of excitement, whether it is but the hysterical excitement of the women over the pigs, or some primary passion. Once indeed, the hidden passion instead of finding expression by its choice among the passions of others, shows itself

16

in the most direct way of all, that of dream. 'Last night,' he writes, at Innismaan, 'after walking in a dream among buildings with strangely intense light on them, I heard a faint rhythm of music beginning far away on some stringed instrument.

It came closer to me, gradually increasing in quickness and volume with an irresistibly definite progression. When it was quite near the sound began to move in my nerves and blood, to urge me to dance with them.

I knew that if I yielded I would be carried away into some moment of terrible agony, so I struggled to remain quiet, holding my knees together with my hands.

The music increased continually, sounding like the strings of harps tuned to a forgotten scale, and having a resonance as searching as the strings of the 'cello.

Then the luring excitement became more powerful than my will, and my limbs moved in spite of me.

In a moment I was swept away in a whirlwind of notes. My breath and my thoughts and every impulse of my body became a form of the dance, till I could not distinguish between the instrument or the rhythm and my own person or consciousness. For a while it seemed an excitement that was filled with joy; then it grew into an ecstasy where all existence was lost in the vortex of movement. I could not think that there had been a life beyond the whirling of the dance.

Then with a shock, the ecstasy turned to agony and rage. I struggled to free myself but seemed only to increase the passion of the steps I moved to. When I shrieked I could only echo the notes of the rhythm. At last, with a movement of uncontrollable frenzy I broke back to consciousness and awoke.

I dragged myself trembling to the window of the cottage and looked out. The moon was glittering across the bay and there was no sound anywhere on the island.'

XIII.

In all drama which would give direct expression to reverie, to the speech of the soul with itself, there is some device that checks the rapidity of dialogue. When Oedipus speaks out of the most vehement passions, he is conscious of the presence of the chorus, men before whom he must keep up appearances 'children latest born of Cadmus' line' who do not share his passion. Nobody is hurried or breathless. We listen to reports and discuss them, taking part as it were in a council of state. Nothing happens before our eyes. The dignity of Greek drama, and in a lesser degree of that of Corneille and Racine depends, as contrasted with the troubled life of Shakespearean drama, on an almost even speed of dialogue, and on a so continuous exclusion of the animation of common life, that thought remains lofty and language rich. Shakespeare, upon whose stage everything may happen, even the blinding of Gloster, and who has no formal check except what is implied in the slow, elaborate structure of blank verse, obtains time for reverie by an often encumbering Euphuism, and by such a loosening of his plot as will give his characters the leisure to look at life from without. Maeterlinck, to name the first modern of the old way who comes to mind--reaches the same end, by choosing instead of human beings persons who are as faint as a breath upon a looking-glass, symbols who can speak a language slow and heavy with dreams because their own life is but a dream. Modern drama, on the other hand, which accepts the tightness of the classic plot, while expressing life directly, has been driven to make indirect its expression of the mind, which it leaves to be inferred from some common-place sentence or gesture as we infer it in ordinary life; and this is, I believe, the cause of the perpetual disappointment of the hope imagined this hundred years that France or Spain or Germany or Scandinavia will at last produce the master we await.

The divisions in the arts are almost all in the first instance technical, and the great schools of drama have been divided from one another by the form or the metal of their mirror, by the check chosen for the rapidity of dialogue. Synge found the check that suited his temperament in an elaboration of the dialects of Kerry and Aran. The cadence is long and meditative, as befits the thought of men who are much alone, and who when they meet in one another's houses--as their way is at the day's end--listen patiently, each man speaking in turn and for some little time, and taking pleasure in the vaguer meaning of the words and in their sound. Their thought, when not merely practical, is as full of traditional wisdom and extravagant pictures as that of some Aeschylean chorus, and no matter what the topic is, it is as though the present were held at arms length. It is the reverse of rhetoric, for the speaker serves his own delight, though doubtless he would tell you that like Raftery's whiskey- drinking it was but for the company's sake. A medicinal manner of speech too, for it could not even express, so little abstract it is and so rammed with life, those worn generalizations of national propaganda. 'I'll be telling you the finest story you'd hear any place from Dundalk to Ballinacree with great queens in it, making themselves matches from the start to the end, and they with shiny silks on them ... I've a grand story of the great queens of Ireland, with white necks on them the like of Sarah Casey, and fine arms would hit you a slap.... What good am I this night, God help me? What good are the grand stories I have when it's few would listen to an old woman, few but a girl maybe would be in great fear the time her hour was come, or a little child wouldn't be sleeping with the hunger on a cold night.' That has the flavour of Homer, of the Bible, of Villon, while Cervantes would have thought it sweet in the mouth though not his food. This use of Irish dialect for noble purpose by Synge, and by Lady Gregory, who had it already in her Cuchulain of Muirthemne, and by Dr. Hyde in those first translations he has not equalled since, has done much for National dignity. When I was a boy I was often troubled and sorrowful because Scottish dialect was capable of noble use, but the Irish of obvious roystering humour only; and this error fixed on my imagination by so many novelists and rhymers made me listen badly. Synge wrote down words and phrases wherever he went, and with that knowledge of Irish which made all our country idioms easy to his hand, found it so rich a thing, that he had begun translating into it fragments of the great literatures of the world, and had planned a complete version of the Imitation of Christ. It gave him imaginative richness and yet left to him the sting and tang of reality. How vivid in his translation from Villon are those 'eyes with a big gay look out of them would bring folly from a great scholar.' More vivid surely than anything in Swinburne's version, and how noble those words which are yet simple country speech, in which his Petrarch mourns that death came upon Laura just as time was making chastity easy, and the day come when 'lovers may sit together and say out all things arc in their hearts,' and 'my sweet enemy was making a start, little by little, to give over her great wariness, the way she was wringing a sweet thing out of my sharp sorrow.'

XIV.

Once when I had been saying that though it seemed to me that a conventional descriptive passage encumbered the action at the moment of crisis. I liked 'The Shadow of the Glen' better than 'Riders to the Sea' that is, for all the nobility of its end, its mood of Greek tragedy, too passive in suffering; and had quoted from Matthew Arnold's introduction to 'Empedocles on Etna,' Synge answered, 'It is a curious thing that "The Riders to the Sea" succeeds with an English but not with an Irish audience, and "The Shadow of the Glen" which is not liked by an English audience is always liked in Ireland, though it is disliked there in theory.' Since then 'The Riders to the Sea' has grown into great popularity in Dublin, partly because with the tactical instinct of an Irish mob, the demonstrators against 'The Playboy' both in the press and in the theatre, where it began the evening, selected it for applause. It is now what Shelley's 'Cloud' was for many years, a comfort to those who do not like to deny altogether the genius they cannot understand. Yet I am certain that, in the long run, his grotesque plays with their lyric beauty, their violent laughter, 'The Playboy of the Western World' most of all, will be loved for holding so much of the mind of Ireland. Synge has written of 'The Playboy' 'anyone who has lived in real intimacy with the Irish peasantry will know that the wildest sayings in this play are tame indeed compared with the fancies one may hear at any little hillside cottage of Geesala, or Carraroe, or Dingle Bay.' It is the strangest, the most beautiful expression in drama of that Irish fantasy, which overflowing through all Irish Literature that has come out of Ireland itself (compare the fantastic Irish account of the Battle of Clontarf with the sober Norse account) is the unbroken character of Irish genius. In modern days this genius has delighted in mischievous extravagance, like that of the Gaelic poet's curse upon his children, 'There are three things that I hate, the devil that is waiting for my soul, the worms that are waiting for my body, my children, who are waiting for my wealth and care neither for my body nor my soul: Oh, Christ hang all in the same noose!' I think those words were spoken with a delight in their vehemence that took out of anger half the bitterness with all the gloom. An old man on the Aran Islands told me the very tale on which 'The Playboy' is founded, beginning with the words, 'If any gentleman has done a crime we'll hide him. There was a gentleman that killed his father, & I had him in my own house six months till he got away to America.' Despite the solemnity of his slow speech his eyes shone as the eyes must have shone in that Trinity College branch of the Gaelic League, which began every meeting with prayers for the death of an old Fellow of College who disliked their movement, or as they certainly do when patriots are telling how short a time the prayers took to the killing of him. I have seen a crowd, when certain Dublin papers had wrought themselves into an imaginary loyalty, so possessed by what seemed the very genius of satiric fantasy, that one all but looked to find some feathered heel among the cobble stones. Part of the delight of crowd or individual is always that somebody will be angry, somebody take the sport for gloomy earnest.

We are mocking at his solemnity, let us therefore so hide our malice that he may be more solemn still, and the laugh run higher yet. Why should we speak his language and so wake him from a dream of all those emotions which men feel because they should, and not because they must? Our minds, being sufficient to themselves, do not wish for victory but are content to elaborate our extravagance, if fortune aid, into wit or lyric beauty, and as for the rest 'There are nights when a king like Conchobar would spit upon his arm-ring and queens will stick out their tongues at the rising moon.' This habit of the mind has made Oscar Wilde and Mr. Bernard Shaw the most celebrated makers of comedy to our time, and if it has sounded plainer still in the conversation of the one, and in some few speeches of the other, that is but because they have not been able to turn out of their plays an alien trick of zeal picked up in struggling youth. Yet, in Synge's plays also, fantasy gives the form and not the thought, for the core is always as in all great art, an over-powering vision of certain virtues, and our capacity for sharing in that vision is the measure of our delight. Great art chills us at first by its coldness or its strangeness, by what seems capricious, and yet it is from these qualities it has authority, as though it had fed on locust and wild honey. The imaginative writer shows us the world as a painter does his picture, reversed in a looking-glass that we may see it, not as it seems to eyes habit has made dull, but as we were Adam and this the first morning; and when the new image becomes as little strange as the old we shall stay with him, because he has, beside the strangeness, not strange to him, that made us share his vision, sincerity that makes us share his feeling.

To speak of one's emotions without fear or moral ambition, to come out from under the shadow of other men's minds, to forget their needs, to be utterly oneself, that is all the Muses care for. Villon, pander, thief, and man-slayer, is as immortal in their eyes, and illustrates in the cry of his ruin as great a truth as Dante in abstract ecstasy, and touches our compassion more. All art is the disengaging of a soul from place and history, its suspension in a beautiful or terrible light, to await the Judgement, and yet, because all its days were a Last Day, judged already. It may show the crimes of Italy as Dante did, or Greek mythology like Keats, or Kerry and Galway villages, and so vividly that ever after I shall look at all with like eyes, and yet I know that Cino da Pistoia thought Dante unjust, that Keats knew no Greek, that those country men and women are neither so lovable nor so lawless as 'mine author sung it me;' that I have added to my being, not my knowledge.

XV.

I wrote the most of these thoughts in my diary on the coast of Normandy, and as I finished came upon Mont Saint Michel, and thereupon doubted for a day the foundation of my school. Here I saw the places of assembly, those cloisters on the rock's summit, the church, the great halls where monks, or knights, or men at arms sat at meals, beautiful from ornament or proportion. I remembered ordinances of the Popes forbidding drinking- cups with stems of gold to these monks who had but a bare dormitory to sleep in. Even when imagining, the individual had taken more from his fellows and his fathers than he gave; one man finishing what another had begun; and all that majestic fantasy, seeming more of Egypt than of Christendom, spoke nothing to the solitary soul, but seemed to announce whether past or yet to come an heroic temper of social men, a bondage of adventure and of wisdom. Then I thought more patiently and I saw that what had made these but as one and given them for a thousand years the miracles of their shrine and temporal rule by land and sea, was not a condescension to knave or dolt, an impoverishment of the common thought to make it serviceable and easy, but a dead language and a communion in whatever, even to the greatest saint, is of incredible difficulty. Only by the substantiation of the soul I thought, whether in literature or in sanctity, can we come upon those agreements, those separations from all else that fasten men together lastingly; for while a popular and picturesque Burns and Scott can but create a province, and our Irish cries and grammars serve some passing need, Homer, Shakespeare, Dante, Goethe and all who travel in their road with however poor a stride, define races and create everlasting loyalties. Synge, like all of the great kin, sought for the race, not through the eyes or in history, or even in the future, but where those monks found God, in the depths of the mind, and in all art like his, although it does not command--indeed because it does not--may lie the roots of far-branching events. Only that which does not teach, which does not cry out, which does not persuade, which does not condescend, which does not explain is irresistible. It is made by men who expressed themselves to the full, and it works through the best minds; whereas the external and picturesque and declamatory writers, that they may create kilts and bagpipes and newspapers and guide-books, leave the best minds empty, and in Ireland and Scotland England runs into the hole. It has no array of arguments and maxims, because the great and the simple (and the Muses have never known which of the two most pleases them) need their deliberate thought for the day's work, and yet will do it worse if they have not grown into or found about them, most perhaps in the minds of women, the nobleness of emotion, associated with the scenery and events of their country, by those great poets, who have dreamed it in solitude, and who to this day in Europe are creating indestructible spiritual races, like those religion has created in the East.

W. B. Yeats.

September 14th. 1910.

WITH SYNGE IN CONNEMARA

I had often spent a day walking with John Synge, but a year or two ago I travelled for a month alone through the west of Ireland with him. He was the best companion for a roadway any one could have, always ready and always the same; a bold walker, up hill and down dale, in the hot sun and the pelting rain. I remember a deluge on the Erris Peninsula, where we lay among the sand hills and at his suggestion heaped sand upon ourselves to try and keep dry.

When we started on our journey, as the train steamed out of Dublin, Synge said: 'Now the elder of us two should be in command on this trip.' So we compared notes and I found that he was two months older than myself. So he was boss and whenever it was a question whether we should take the road to the west or the road to the south, it was Synge who finally decided.

Synge was fond of little children and animals. I remember how glad he was to stop and lean on a wall in Gorumna and watch a woman in afield shearing a sheep. It was an old sheep and must have often been sheared before by the same hand, for the woman hardly held it; she just knelt beside it and snipped away. I remember the sheep raised its lean old head to look at the stranger, and the woman just put her hand on its cheek and gently pressed its head down on the grass again.

Synge was delighted with the narrow paths made of sods of grass alongside the newly-metalled roads, because he thought they had been put there to make soft going for the bare feet of little children. Children knew, I think, that he wished them well. In Bellmullet on Saint John's eve, when we stood in the market square watching the fire-play, flaming sods of turf soaked in paraffine, hurled to the sky and caught and skied again, and burning snakes of hay-rope, I remember a little girl in the crowd, in an ecstasy of pleasure and dread, clutched Synge by the hand and stood close in his shadow until the fiery games were done.

His knowledge of Gaelic was a great assistance to him in talking to the people. I remember him holding a great conversation in Irish and English with an innkeeper's wife in a Mayo inn. She had lived in America in Lincoln's day. She told us what living cost in America then, and of her life there; her little old husband sitting by and putting in an odd word. By the way, the husband was a wonderful gentle-mannered man, for we had luncheon in his house of biscuits and porter, and rested there an hour, waiting for a heavy shower to blow away; and when we said good-bye and our feet were actually on the road, Synge said, 'Did we pay for what we had?' So I called back to the innkeeper, 'Did we pay you?' and he said quietly, 'Not yet sir.'

Synge was always delighted to hear and remember any good phrase. I remember his delight at the words of a local politician who told us how he became a Nationalist. 'I was,' he said plucking a book from the mantlepiece (I remember the book--it was 'Paul and Virginia') and clasping it to his breast--'I was but a little child with my little book going to school, and by the house there I saw the agent. He took the unfortunate tenant and thrun him in the road, and I saw the man's wife come out crying and the agent's wife thrun her in the channel, and when I saw that, though I was but a child, I swore I'd be a Nationalist. I swore by heaven, and I swore by hell and all the rivers that run through them.'

Synge must have read a great deal at one time, but he was not a man you would see often with a book in his hand; he would sooner talk, or rather listen to talk-- almost anyone's talk.

Synge was always ready to go anywhere with one, and when there to enjoy what came. He went with me to see an ordinary melodrama at the Queen's Theatre, Dublin, and he delighted to see how the members of the company could by the vehemence of their movements and the resources of their voices hold your attention on a play where everything was commonplace. He enjoyed seeing the contrite villain of the piece come up from the bottom of the gulch, hurled there by the adventuress, and flash his sweating blood-stained face up against the footlights; and, though he told us he had but a few short moments to live, roar his contrition with the voice of a bull.

Synge had travelled a great deal in Italy in tracks he beat out for himself, and in Germany and in France, but he only occasionally spoke to me about these places. I think the Irish peasant had all his heart. He loved them in the east as well as he loved them in the west, but the western men on the Aran Islands and in the Blaskets fitted in with his humour more than any; the wild things they did and said were a joy to him.

Synge was by spirit well equipped for the roads. Though his health was often bad, he had beating under his ribs a brave heart that carried him over rough tracks. He gathered about him very little gear, and cared nothing for comfort except perhaps that of a good turf fire. He was, though young in years, 'an old dog for a hard road and not a young pup for a tow-path.'

He loved mad scenes. He told me how once at the fair of Tralee he saw an old tinker-woman taken by the police, and she was struggling with them in the centre of the fair; when suddenly, as if her garments were held together with one cord, she hurled every shred of clothing from her, ran down the street and screamed, 'let this be the barrack yard,' which was perfectly understood by the crowd as suggesting that the police strip and beat their prisoners when they get them shut in, in the barrack yard. The young men laughed, but the old men hurried after the naked fleeting figure trying to throw her clothes on her as she ran.

But all wild sights appealed to Synge, he did not care whether they were typical of anything else or had any symbolical meaning at all. If he had lived in the days of piracy he would have been the fiddler in a pirate- schooner, him they called 'the music--' 'The music' looked on at every thing with dancing eyes but drew no sword, and when the schooner was taken and the pirates hung at Cape Corso Castle or The Island of Saint Christopher's, 'the music' was spared because he *was* 'the music.'

Jack B. Yeats

CPSIA information can be obtained at www.ICGtesting.com
Printed in the USA
BVOW03s1125180414

351057BV00015B/403/P

9 781407 649467